PICTURING SCOTLAND

SOUTHERN ARGYLL

NESS PUBLISHING

2 The very south of Southern Argyll: the magnificent sweep of Brunerican and Dunaverty Bays on the southern shore of Kintyre, taken from the road that leads to the Mull of Kintyre. Towards the right of

SOUTHERN ARGYLL

the picture is Dunaverty Head (see p.10) and the headland in the middle of the picture is Keil Point, location of the cave pictured on p.11.

Welcome to Southern Argyll!

In total, the magnificent realm of land and water that is Argyll stretches approximately 120 miles up Scotland's western seaboard, incorporates 26 inhabited islands and is a hotbed of ancient history. Its many sea lochs and islands make Argyll's coastline longer than that of France; its landmass of 6,930 sq. km. makes it larger than Belgium. Due to its size and range, this book will concentrate on the southern reaches, defined as the Kintyre Peninsula, the islands of Gigha, Islay, Jura and Colonsay, Knapdale and south Kilmartin. Within these territories are all the shades of scenery and as many aspects of mankind's influence upon it as anyone could wish to find.

The name 'Argyll' comes from the Gaelic *Earra-Ghaidheal* meaning the boundary of the Gaels. It was indeed frontier territory, for the Gaels, a people of Celtic ethnicity who migrated from Ireland, inevitably found other peoples already established. Nevertheless, by about 500AD they were able to establish the kingdom of Dál Riata in Argyll. This name was taken from that which already applied to a kingdom based on present-day County Antrim in Northern Ireland. When the seat of kingship was moved to Dunadd at the southern end of Kilmartin glen, this hill fort became the most important place in their realm. Following Irish tradition, a footprint was carved in a flat rock on Dunadd's

Campbeltown, one of the largest towns in Argyll, viewed from across Campbeltown Loch. 5
The tower of Lorne & Lowland Church is prominent on the right.

summit and the king inaugurated by placing his foot into the imprint (see picture on p.1). There are few places in Scotland where one can engage so directly with the country's distant past.

Celtic Christianity came to Scotland as a result of the missionary work of St Columba (521–597) and those who followed him. In 563 he landed on the southern tip of Kintyre where only 12 miles or so separate it from Ireland. The legacy of the early evangelists is still vivid in these parts.

To cover the ground in a reasonably logical way, this book begins at Campbeltown (see previous page and opposite) in the extreme south and works its way up Kintyre. As this involves passing where the ferries head for the islands, we take that hint and next explore Gigha, Islay and Jura. Each of these is remarkable in its own way. Islay, for example, boasts a high density of distilleries (eight of them). Bowmore, its principal settlement, lays claim to being the first planned village in Scotland, founded in 1768. And while Islay is a land that man has largely tamed, neighbouring Jura is one of the wildest of Scotland's inhabited islands. Although broadly similar in size, their population figures reflect this: Islay has a resident population of approximately 3,200 while Jura has around 200!

On returning to the mainland, a northerly trajectory takes in Tarbert (the one on Loch Fyne), Ardrishaig and Lochgilphead, Argyll's County Town. Beyond here our final destinations bring us to the point where the *Northern Argyll* volume in this series takes over. The remaining, eastern, part of Argyll is covered in a third book, *Loch Lomond, Cowal & Bute*.

But now, let this photographic journey remind you of or prepare you for the best that this impressive land has to show. Whether your interest lies in trekking up mountains like the Paps of Jura, soaking up the splendour of castles such as Skipness or Sween, delving into the misty past or stretching out on those fabulous beaches, let the exploration begin!

On the left is Campbeltown Library and Museum, also known as the Burnet Building, and on the right the Picture House, one of Scotland's earliest purpose-built cinemas.

8   Dawn over Campbeltown Loch with Davaar Island in the centre. It can only be accessed at low tide, via a mile-long causeway from the mainland. One good reason to visit the island is Archibald

MacKinnon's cave painting of the crucifixion, a work he did in secret in 1887, creating something of a mystery locally. MacKinnon, a local artist, claimed the painting in 1934.

10 This rocky outcrop was the setting for Dunaverty Castle, a fortified site for over 1,000 years from around 500AD. It is near the village of Southend.

This is the entrance to and the inside of Keil Cave at Keil Point, a shelter for our **11** prehistoric ancestors. St Columba landed in this area on his arrival from Ireland in 563.

12 The final stage of the road to Mull of Kintyre lighthouse snakes dramatically down a height of 335m/1100ft. The lighthouse dates back to 1788.

Machrihanish, five miles west of Campbeltown, is noted for its fine beach, first-class golf course and 13
is to be one of 11 strategic Scottish hubs in manufacturing and maintaining offshore wind turbines.

14 The view north from Machrihanish: a host of seabirds pass the time on a skerry just off the beach with a backdrop of the Paps of Jura in the far distance. We'll see more of the Paps later.

About 10 miles up the east coast of Kintyre from Campbeltown is Saddell Abbey, believed to have **15** been founded in 1148. It is home to 12 late-medieval carved stones, including six grave slabs.

16 Continuing up the east side of Kintyre we come to this view which looks across the mouth of Carradale Bay with the Isle of Arran hills in the background.

Over on the west side of Kintyre is Glenbarr Abbey which houses the Clan MacAlister Centre. It is
open to the public from Easter to mid October. Clan MacAlister is an offshoot (sept) of Clan Donald.

18 Returning to east Kintyre and the village of Grogport, where Kilbrannan Sound is backed by the Isle of Arran. (Arran will feature in a further volume in this series.)

Left: Skipness Castle in north-east Kintyre was begun in the early 13th century, when Argyll was **19** ruled not by Scotland but by Norway. Right: the 16th-century tower house at Skipness.

20 From the top of Skipness Castle's tower house, a view which gives an idea of its setting. In the field towards top left are the ruins of the 13th-century St Brendan's Chapel.

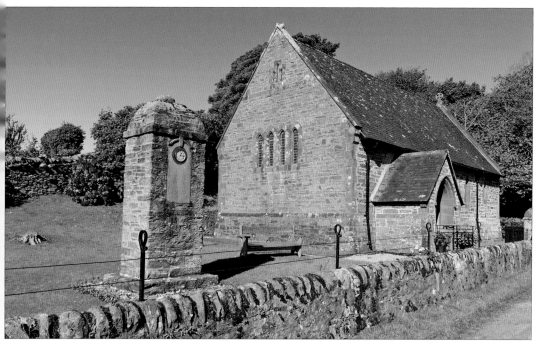

And this is its charming 19th-century replacement in Gothic Revival style, the still-active 21 St Brendan's Church of Scotland kirk.

22 Over on the western side of Kintyre there are miles of glorious beaches like this one, at A'Chleit south of the village of Tayinloan, from where a ferry crosses to the Isle of Gigha.

And over on Gigha ('God's Island'), these two views capture something of what there is **23** to see at Achamore Gardens.

24 This glorious panorama looks north from Kintyre over West Loch Tarbert and into Knapdale.
The ferry on the right is berthed at the small port of Kennacraig from where it will sail to the

islands of Islay and Colonsay. So we'll take the hint and head next for Islay (pronounced Ila). **25**

26 However, before Islay another look at Gigha and the exquisite little Ardminish bay. The crowd on the beach are enjoying some live music, part of the Gigha Music Festival.

If taking the ferry from Kennacraig to Port Ellen, a scene like this will be your first impression of the **27**
island of Islay. Port Ellen is the main settlement on the south of Islay.

28 It is said that Islay has whisky in its soul, with no fewer than eight working distilleries. Laphroaig, just east of Port Ellen, is one of them, famed for its peaty malt whiskies.

Dunyvaig Castle, overlooking Lagavulin Bay, was a fortress of the MacDonald Lords of the Isles built **29** to protect their fleet, and the castle ruins are still prominent today.

30 Lagavulin is the next in a line of distilleries east of Port Ellen. It officially dates from 1816, though records show illicit distillation on the site as far back as 1742.

Left: Kildalton Cross, on the south-east corner of Islay, is the finest intact high cross in Scotland, carved **31** in the late 8th century. Right: The ruins of Kildalton Church provide some interesting perspectives.

32 Ardbeg is the third in the line of distilleries east of Port Ellen. After being 'mothballed' in 1981, it was reopened in 1997 and is now one of the fastest growing Islay malts.

Islay has a wonderful coastline of great variety. Not surprisingly this beach is simply called **33**
Big Strand and stretches along the six miles of Laggan Bay north of Port Ellen.

34 This is Bowmore, Islay's principal town and administrative capital. This view looks up Main Street from the harbour to the Round Church, parish church of Kilarrow, built in 1767.

The church's beautiful interior: the story goes that it was built in a circular shape to make sure there were no corners for the devil to hide in!

36 Left: Bowmore Distillery is situated in the centre of the town; it is the oldest legal distillery on Islay.
Right: Another face of Islay's coast where sea erosion has created this double rock arch.

Yes, another distillery! Each of Islay's eight distilleries has its own character, in this case a novel way **37** of proclaiming its name. Bruichladdich is on the opposite side of Loch Indaal from Bowmore.

38 A couple of miles on from Bruichladdich is the charming village of Port Charlotte, home of the Islay Life Museum, a 'must' for visitors to the island.

At the end of the road down the Rhinns of Islay is Portnahaven. The sheltered harbour is a **39** well-known resting place for many seals, which seem quite happy to pose for the camera.

40 Picturesque Portnahaven is a planned village, a product of the 19th century, with fishing and
crofting as the main sources of employment for the villagers. Nowadays there can be few better spots

on the island for those looking for peace and quiet, whether for a holiday or a more permanent abode.

42 Port Wemyss is Portnahaven's neighbouring village, from where this image captures some of the local colour and, across the bay, Orsay Island and the 1825-built Rhinns of Islay lighthouse.

Islay's coast close to Port Wemyss on a day when it shows its stormier side, but harsh weather **43** makes for dramatic scenes.

44 Moving north up Islay's west coast to Sanaig, tranquillity has returned and the combination of pink-flowering Thrift, a perfect sky and aquamarine sea are so inviting.

At Bolsa, near the northern tip of Islay, another of nature's wonderful combinations of colour and **45** form mark the end of another island day.

46 The island's fauna and flora are a reason many people would give for visiting Islay. Left: seeing an otter is always a thrill. Right: flowers such as these Pyramidal Orchids are also an attraction.

The medieval ruins at Finlaggan, at one time the main centre of power for the Lordship of the Isles, **47**
on an island in the beautiful secluded Loch Finlaggan in the north-east corner of Islay.

48 Our journey around Islay ends at Port Askaig in the north-east of the island where a colourful array of fishing boats await their next duties.

From the departing ferry, this is the Port Askaig Hotel. A crossing of a few minutes over the **49**
Sound of Islay takes travellers to the Isle of Jura.

50 Left: the small ferry has to cope with strong currents in the narrow sound. Right: first stop on Jura is Jura House Gardens where the resident birds are tame enough to be fed by hand.

A 'peephole' view of some of the exotic plants at Jura House Gardens. **51**

52 The classic winter view of Jura with the Paps looking inviting and intimidating in equal measure under a hefty covering of snow.

Jura Distillery, in the village of Craighouse, was established in 1810 and reconstructed in 1963. **53**
It is open most of the year for tours and tastings.

54 Craighouse Bay is one of those places where you just want to sit and watch and pass the time. On the horizon, Beinn Shiantaidh gently suggests that there is also some exercise to be had.

The sheltered eastern coast of Jura generally enjoys a mild climate, allowing the growth of palm trees **55** which add a tropical touch to scenes like this.

56 Jura, with the Paps on the right, captured from the lonely mainland outpost of Keillmore, at the tip of the Tayvallich Peninsula.

58 A visit to Jura is greatly enhanced by an exploration of the three Paps. Straight ahead is Beinn a' Chaolais, at 734m/2407ft the third highest of the three main peaks. Beinn an Oir is on the right.

Left: Beinn Shiantaidh, the Sacred Mountain, is second highest at 757m/2477ft. **59**
Right: deer are plentiful on Jura (over 5,000) and quite likely to be encountered among the hills.

60 The highest of the three is Beinn an Oir, the Mountain of Gold, which reaches 785m/2576ft. This is the magnificent view from its summit, looking north over Jura's wilderness.

Symptomatic of the pace of life on Jura, even the cattle know how to 'chill out' and enjoy the sea. **61**

62 Further up Jura's eastern seaboard, another dose of tranquillity and beauty waits for those who find delightful Ardlussa Bay.

The Isle of Colonsay lies about eight miles west of Jura and has its own store of delights, **63** such as this azalea garden at Colonsay House. (See the back cover for another view of Colonsay.)

64 Back on the mainland once again, 'messing about in boats' is clearly the order of the day at Tarbert, situated on the isthmus that attaches Kintyre to the rest of Argyll.

Tarbert is an attractive town and harbour (see also the front cover picture) which can look as **65** enchanting by night as by day. This has been a place of shelter for at least a thousand years.

66 Continuing north from Tarbert we come to Ardrishaig and the eastern end of the Crinan Canal. It was built to provide a shortcut from the Clyde estuary to Hebridean waters.

Lochgilphead stands at the head of Loch Gilp, a small loch on the west side of Loch Fyne. The town **67** was first laid out as a planned settlement in about 1790 and is Argyll's administrative capital.

68 About three miles from Lochgilphead at Cairnbaan there are several sets of these 'cup-and-ring' markings. Simple but intriguing, as they were made about 5,000 years ago and their purpose is uncertain.

Beavers were released in Knapdale Forest during May 2009 and have settled in well to their new **69** home. The first kits were born in August 2010, one of which is seen here with an adult beaver.

70 At Crinan, where the canal meets the Sound of Jura, the photo opportunities just multiply. Every year, two to three thousand vessels, mostly pleasure craft, pass through here.

Looking north from the village across Loch Crinan provides this enticing view, enriched by the **71** autumn colours. The house is in an idyllic but remote location.

72 Left: the canal basin at Crinan always seems to be hosting some lovely old boats, sometimes including

(right) VIC (Victualling Inshore Craft) 32, one of the last survivors of a series of steam 'puffers'.

74 From Crinan we venture south into Knapdale to find the remote village of Tayvallich. Sited by a bay on Loch Sween, it is a particularly well sheltered haven.

Keeping right on to the end of the road in this part of Knapdale takes us to the Island of Danna, **75** from where this long range view reaches Ben Cruachan in northern Argyll, about 40 miles away.

76 From the same vantage point but looking east is Castle Sween, across the loch of the same name. It is the oldest standing castle in Scotland, built by Sven The Red in the 12th century.

Our final stop on this journey is the hill fort of Dunadd in the south of Kilmartin Glen. This was once one of the most important places in (what became) Scotland. 77

78 From about 500 to 900 this 175ft-high outcrop was where the kings of Dál Riata were anointed. The picture shows part of the way to the summit, showing what a defensible place it was.

In the foreground is a remnant of the fortifications. From here we enter Northern Argyll where **79** the journey continues in the accompanying volume in this series ...

Published 2011 by Ness Publishing, 47 Academy Street, Elgin, Moray, IV30 1LR
Phone 01343 549663   www.nesspublishing.co.uk

All photographs © Colin and Eithne Nutt except p.13 © Scotavia Images; pp.31 (right), 49, 59 (right) & 61
© Sue M. Cleave; pp.33, 36 (right), 38, 43-46, & 52 © Becky Williamson; p.63 & back cover © Colonsay Estate;
p.69 © Steve Gardner/SWT

Text © Colin Nutt
ISBN 978-1-906549-15-2

Front cover: Tarbert, Loch Fyne; p.1: King's footprint, Dunadd; p.4: Chaffinch at Jura House Gardens;
this page: Himalayan Blue Poppy; back cover: Sir John's Pool, Colonsay

For a list of websites and phone numbers please turn over >

Websites and phone numbers (where available) for principal places featured in this book in order of appearance:

Argyll: www.argyllonline.co.uk
www.visitscottishheartlands.com/areas

Campbeltown: www.campbeltown.org.uk

Saddell Abbey: www.argyll-bute.gov.uk

Clan MacAlister Centre: www.glenbarrabbey.com (T) 01583 421247

Skipness Castle: www.historic-scotland.gov.uk

Skipness village: www.skipness.info

Isle of Gigha: www.gigha.org.uk

Isle of Islay: www.islayinfo.com

Laphroaig Distillery: www.Laphroaig.com (T) 01496 302418

Lagavulin Distillery: www.discovering-distilleries.com (T) 01496 302400

Kildalton Cross: www.historic-scotland.gov.uk

Ardbeg Distillery: www.ardbeg.com (T) 01496 302244

Bowmore Distillery: www.bowmore.co.uk (T) 01496 810441

Bruichladdich Distillery: www.bruichladdich.com (T) 01496 850221

Isle of Jura: www.jurainfo.com

Jura House and Gardens: www.jurahouseandgardens.co.uk